The Unseen

Copyright © 2025 by Yesmar Holistic Health Center. All rights reserved.

Published by: Yesmar Holistic Health Center LLC.

This book is based on a true story. The characters and events are a representation of a narrative of a deep friendship.

No part of this publication may be reproduced, distributed, or transmitted in any form or by any means, including photocopying, recording, or other electronic or mechanical methods, without the prior written permission of the publisher, except in the case of brief quotations embodied in critical reviews and certain other noncommercial uses permitted by copyright law.

ISBN: 9798298760652

For permission requests, write to the publisher at: info@yesmarholistic.com

Table of Contents

The Unseen Medicine of a Sacred Man 3

Chapter 1: The Sanctuary of Broken Men 5

Chapter 2: The Sound of One's Own Drum 10

Chapter 3: The Plumb Line of the Soul 14

Chapter 4: The House Built on Sand 16

Chapter 5: A Good Heart's Sunlight 20

Chapter 6: The Final Smoke 23

Saying #1: The World's sweet poison offers visions of madness. 27

Saying #2: Beat to the rhythm of your own drum, for every living thing has its own song. 29

Saying #3: Impure motives poison all things. . 31

Saying #4: A good heart is sunlight for others. 33

Saying #5: A good heart is a warrior's choice. 35

Saying #6: The word is a powerful force for creation and healing. 36

Saying #7: Belief is a matter of survival, a living thing. 37

Saying #8: Freedom is a sacred dance on the path of truth. 38

The Unseen Medicine of a Sacred Man

This is based on a true story.

It is a narrative of a Black therapist and a Native American elder, a chronicle of an unlikely friendship forged not in an office, but in the quiet of a Waffle House booth. A novice counselor, trained in textbook therapy, finds his life's purpose utterly upended by a man the world had long ago written off—a homeless, friendless elder with a history of incarceration and a spirit weighed down by trauma. But the elder's wisdom defies conventional frameworks. He teaches with a prophet's weary certainty and a warrior's resolve, revealing the path to a pure heart, the true meaning of freedom, and the creative power of a spoken word. Over stale coffee and cigarette smoke, he delivers a masterclass in living, forcing the therapist to confront his own hypocrisies and find the courage to walk his own sacred path.

This story is a journey into the heart of ancestral pain and the unyielding resilience of the human spirit. It is a testament to the idea that the greatest lessons are often found in the most unexpected places, from those who are tired of talking but are desperate to be heard.

Chapter 1: The Sanctuary of Broken Men

I was a provisional counselor and a novice therapist, a Black man navigating a world that felt foreign to me, working at a Native American resource center. I had been hired to provide mental health services to Native participants, and I was diligently learning about Native ways such as Wellbriety to provide culturally appropriate care. But I felt like an imposter, an outsider. My life had been shaped by people the world had written off—outcasts and the seemingly friendless. Yet, here I was, an outsider, trained to help a community whose history of forced displacement, broken treaties, and intergenerational trauma was not my own. I was the one who felt I didn't belong.

Our paths first crossed in the center's office, a space that felt stiff and unwelcoming. My patient was a man who had spent decades incarcerated, was estranged from his family, friendless, and suffering from PTSD. He carried a deep-seated distrust for any institution, especially those connected to the government. His face, a testament to a life lived hard—hard labor, long miles, and sleepless nights—showed the weariness of a man who had walked a thousand miles for every destination. It was a roadmap of a man perpetually in motion, who had been incarcerated for decades and had since sheltered in homeless camps and done odd jobs for a ride or a temporary stay. Nothing was ever easy.

We both knew we needed a different kind of space, one where he could truly be himself. The idea of him "professing his feelings" in that sterile office was an insult to the life he had lived. So, we made a pact to meet every week at a Waffle House. The diner became our sanctuary, a place he chose because it provided a sense of safety and belonging. Here, he was not an "invisible homeless guy," but a welcomed and included person whose deep wisdom and unique personality shone through with each passing week.

That first week, as I watched him from my car before going in, my mind raced. My own institutional training felt laughably inadequate. How could my textbooks possibly prepare me for a man who carried centuries of history in his posture and a lifetime of personal pain in his eyes? My own history, the trauma of African slavery and its long, lingering shadow on my family, felt like a silent dialogue with his. I had learned how generations of trauma can be passed down, affecting health, family dynamics, and a person's very sense of purpose. I felt an old connection, a shared understanding of a society that paid lip service to poverty, while systematically stripping people of their liberty and identity.

I walked in, a novice therapist with a carefully constructed smile. I tried to apply a textbook technique, a question about his feelings, but he deflected it with a wry smirk. I quickly realized my mistake; his wisdom and personality defied conventional therapeutic frameworks. So, I simply listened. He spoke of his decades in prison, of a family that was now a collection of strangers, and of the PTSD that haunted his days. He was a man who had spent years fighting a system he believed was fundamentally corrupt. Yet, he had come to me because he was thinking of dying by suicide, a quiet battle he fought daily.

The Waffle House air was thick with the scent of stale coffee and Marlboro cigarettes. Most would find it unpleasant, but to me, it was the smell of a sacred man. The tobacco he loved is a sacred plant in Native culture, so while it seemed to others that he reeked of cigarette smoke, to me, he was all spirit. He had a sharp tongue for injustice but a gentle heart for those in need. He was a man who cried when he smiled and told jokes in the same breath. He was also a man who spoke of the world's impending doom with a weary certainty. He almost went through with it once, until he saw a dove outside his window. He believed it was a sign from God. He would cry every time he told me the story, which he did every time we met.

My conversations with him were like a living notebook. After each meeting, I'd find myself in my car, scribbling furiously, trying to capture the essence of a man who was both a walking contradiction and a profound teacher. He would share these pieces of himself, grudgingly at first, as if he felt we didn't deserve his wisdom or his effort because of our selfish ways. Yet, he shared it with me anyway.

Chapter 2: The Sound of One's Own Drum

One week, the topic turned from the pain he carried to the war he had always waged. His demeanor would shift. He would look out the window, his finger a sharp indictment of the world passing by, his voice all but a snarl as he pointed at the roads where animals once roamed free and the telephone poles where birds perched instead of trees. All of this, he said, was the decay caused by materialism.

"What do you gain from fighting it so much?" I asked, my voice as calm as I could make it. "Do you ever regret not playing the game of life on its own terms?"

He turned from the window, his gaze settling on me with a weary certainty. "The world's ways were a 'sweet poison causing hallucinations'," he said, his voice a low whisper as he stirred his coffee. "To play its game is to drink that poison. I lived every day, in the mix of organized religion, government, and commerce. They take your spirit and put it in a box."

I took a slow breath, letting the weight of his words settle. My mind flashed back to my own family's history, to the systems that had tried to put our spirits in a box. I saw the parallels in the forced assimilation, the stripping of identity, the constant push-pull between resistance and survival. I didn't regret my question. I was a novice therapist, but in that moment, I was something more—a man sitting with a history that felt oddly, painfully familiar. I simply nodded, the gesture acknowledging the gravity of what he had revealed, not just about himself, but about the world.

He then spoke of a narrow, often difficult road, but it was the only one that led to true freedom and a life where you could hear the beat of your own drum, clear and strong, without the static of the world's poison.

He would speak of the word, his voice low but powerful. "It is creative a powerful force", he would say. He understood the word not as just communication, but as a tool for creation and healing, much like the ceremonial language of his ancestors. He knew that a prayer, a blessing, or even a spoken truth could shape reality for the better.

I listened, my pen hovering over my notebook. "But you see the sickness in the world," I said, my voice quiet, "and you see the pathway out. You have the knowledge. You have the creative word. Why don't you use it to heal the world you see?"

His demeanor shifted. His eyes, no longer filled with the ancient wisdom he had just offered, filled with a deep, mirrored pain. He looked away, back to the window. His voice, when he spoke, was a low, pained whisper. "I have, in my mind, already condemned this world. I am a healer who refuses to heal, even myself." He turned back to me, his gaze raw and unforgiving. "My own spirit is so pained it cannot find the light for its own wounds. I can see the path, but I can no longer find the strength to walk it."

The air in the diner grew thick with a silence that was heavier than the smell of stale coffee and cigarette smoke. It was the silence of a man who had offered his greatest wisdom, and in doing so, had revealed his deepest, most consuming wound.

Chapter 3: The Plumb Line of the Soul

One morning, he pulled a worn binder from his canvas bag. It was filled with pages on Native American heroes, a school project given to him by a young white girl. He watched me as I slowly turned each page, his gaze unwavering. It was a test of my intentions and spirit. Was I a safe person to know this history, or just another user? He wanted to see if I had the heart to carry his stories.

He pointed to a page on Crazy Horse, a freedom fighter who resisted the reservation system. "He fought for a way of life, not just for land," he said. He then pointed to a page about Charles Eastman (Ohiye S'a), the physician and writer who advocated for his people's rights with his words. "He knew the pen was as strong as the sword," he noted. He saw these heroes not as relics of the past but as living examples of pure intention.

He would then turn his focus to me, his stare

demanding my full attention. "What is leading me?" he would ask. "What do I obey without questions?" He used these questions like a plumb line, a way to weigh his own heart and demand that I weigh mine. He insisted on knowing my motives, knowing what drove me beneath the surface. "Check my motives" he would say, because "Impure motives pollute all things".

I had been trying to do my job well, to be a good therapist, but in that moment, I realized my professional intentions were as flimsy as the veneer of the Waffle House booth. I felt the heat of my own hypocrisy. "I'm not entirely sure," I admitted, my voice barely audible. "I'm still searching. I'm trained to help, but... I don't know what my motive is."

A smirk touched the corner of his mouth; he didn't believe me. He confronted me for asking questions about the world, but not being willing to answer for my own life.

"What on your life requires faith in the unknown and un-seeable?" he challenged.

Chapter 4: The House Built on Sand

It was here that the lessons truly began. He was no longer just talking. He was teaching, his voice taking on the righteous, prophetic tone of a shaman in a sweat lodge, and I was the young man he was molding. I imagined him in full regalia, the smell of tobacco now a sacred ceremonial smoke, as he began to walk me through the teachings.

"The world wants you to believe that a job, a paycheck, a title—those things are your foundation," he said, leaning in. "But that is a house built on sand. They will strip those things away. Your **pure motive** must be to serve, to help others. Because a heart set on power or gain would only produce more of the same sickness in the world. If the root is poisoned, the fruit can never be healthy".

"But that is only the beginning. It is **belief** that is the true foundation. The world has corrupted you, made you a man who says he believes, but waits for things to fall apart".

He was talking about my mother's illness. I had told him about her stage four cancer, about praying for a miracle while also preparing for her death. In his eyes, this was a great hypocrisy. "With one mouth you say you believe, and with the other, you wait for your mother to die. You do not believe!" My academic smarts, my college degree, all fell apart in the presence of a man who understood **true belief**. He said that if you truly believe, she will be healed. He told me that belief, in the Native way, is a matter of survival, a living thing. The Red Road, the path of spiritual living, is not just a path you walk with your feet, but one you walk with every thought, every action. It is a path of truth. "Truth is the only pathway," he'd state bluntly.

"And that truth," he continued, his voice now a powerful crescendo, "is spoken with the **creative word**". He told me of how the ceremonial words of his ancestors could call the rain, how a story could keep a culture alive, how a prayer could restore balance to a world out of nothing but a vision and a voice. He said the word can mend the soul, restore balance, and build a world out of nothing but a vision and a voice.

He paused then, his powerful monologue complete. The diner seemed to shrink around us. I looked at this man, a homeless elder, a man written off by the world, and I saw a teacher who had just given me a masterclass in living. The words I had heard, the ideas I had wrestled with, all came together in a way that my intellect alone could never have achieved. The heat of his words had penetrated my very being.

Tears, hot and unexpected, began to stream down my face. They were not tears of sadness, but of a spiritual release that felt like a new beginning. It was as if a lifetime of my own unspoken burdens, of my people's history, had found a language in his teachings. In the quiet chaos of that Waffle House, a Black man was crying not because he was broken, but because he was finally being put back together.

That evening, I drove home in a daze. The world seemed different, less of a thing to be controlled and more of a living being to be in relationship with. The sterile progress notes I usually drafted felt like a flimsy thing. My work wasn't about mental health diagnoses; it was about spirit. His wisdom became a seed in my mind. I knew, with every fiber of my being, that this man, with his contradictions and his pain, had taught me more than any textbook ever could. I had come to him as a therapist, but I was leaving a student, tasked with carrying a sacred story.

Chapter 5: A Good Heart's Sunlight

One morning, the topic of a good heart arose. He was quieter than usual, his gaze softer, and the usual defiant pride was replaced by a deep well of something else. He spoke of his "sickness," the purposelessness that would "eat you alive from the inside out" but then he found a glimmer of hope. He spoke of his life as a constant struggle, a quiet battle he fought daily. He told me of moments that gave him hope, a way to combat the world's darkness. He spoke of a woman who would give him odd jobs, not for the work, but because her kindness provided a sense of dignity he so rarely found. He spoke of the Waffle House employees who would let him take out the trash for free coffee and a meal. In these small moments, he said, he was not an "invisible homeless guy," but a welcomed and included person.

He talked about the meaning of a good heart, not as a feeling, but as an action. He said that a good heart was the most powerful medicine, and a reminder that even when all else seems lost, the power of love and helping each other remains the only path forward. He then told me a story about his elderly roommate he didn't care much for but needed him. He cared for him because it was a conscious choice to combat the world's darkness by being a source of light for others. He mentored youth he worked with, but only those who cared to listen, because that generation is hard-headed. He had a constant struggle, feeling purposeless and contemplating suicide as a path to freedom from a world he didn't feel he belonged in. He believed that the only antidote to this sickness was a "good heart". He called it "sunlight for others".

His gentleness, which you witnessed when he saw a need, was a direct expression of this belief. It was a conscious choice to combat the world's darkness by being a source of light for others.

I asked him then, "If you could have one thing, what would it be?"

He didn't hesitate. His body, old and breaking, became tough, his face hardening. "Freedom." An ironic thing to say of a man who seemed more free than any I had met prior. But he had so much regret and a fear of re-incarceration. He talked often of re-offending, of rebelling against the world system in a final fight, maybe to get shot by the police. The rage was in his eyes, a fire that had not yet gone out. But he said, a weary certainty in his voice, that his "good heart" prevented it. It was a raging war in his spirit, but his actions, his choices, were a testament to the power of a good heart, and a reminder that even when all else seems lost, the power of love and helping each other remains the only path forward.

Chapter 6: The Final Smoke

He chose to have our last talks beside my car, away from the watchful eyes of the diner. He lit a cigarette, the smoke curling around his face. Here, a different man emerged. His usual defiant pride was gone, replaced by a deep fretting. His shoulders, usually set so straight and proud, were hunched. He never wanted the world to see his weakness, although he cried often, but here, in the quiet of the parking lot, he let it show.

He talked about how in the native way, generational knowledge was shared through a trusted connection. He had intentionally chosen me. He told me I was the child who "would finally listen." He spoke of the Waffle House workers who "seemed to care," seeing in their simple kindness a flicker of hope that the sickness hadn't completely consumed the world.

He confessed to me a sense of overwhelming guilt, that maybe trying to live free for so long was a mistake. He looked at his own state—homeless, jobless—and his voice was low with a crushing humility. "It seems everything he had to do in life he didn't want to but had to survive." He was still in a kind of prison in his mind. He looked at me with a rare vulnerability, his watery eyes searching for a reflection of the wisdom he gave so freely. He had chosen me to be the one to carry his story. He liked me, he liked talking to me. Our friendship was an odd but needed one. The world would be losing something amazing if he died quietly like a tree in the forest and yet only I seemed to know.

To care. His words were a gift, a way to keep him alive in the old way, by sharing his story and his wisdom with the world. He finished the last drag of his cigarette and looked at the minivan parked at the curb. His ride was always there, waiting on him to finish talking to me. He gave a final, solemn nod of his head, a gesture of deep closure. Without another word, he opened the passenger door and got in. As the minivan pulled away, he looked back at me and smiled—a soft, knowing curve of his lips. Then, he was gone. I never saw him again.

The Indian center closed its doors two weeks later. The suddenness of the closure felt like a familiar injustice, a new kind of abuse—suddenly stripped of critical aid at the most inopportune time. My heart sank. I worried about him. Had the world finally become too much for his old brain and shoulders? Had my sessions done any good at all?

I sat in my car, staring at the empty space where the minivan had been. I pulled out my notebook, its pages filled with his sayings. I remember the pain in his eyes when he talked of being an "invisible homeless guy," the irony that a man with so much wisdom could be so overlooked. The world, I realized, was filled with people whose stories were buried by their circumstances, their value lost to the systems that broke them. It would be an unforgivable injustice to let his wisdom disappear. I remembered my vow to make sure he was not forgotten.

This is the story I am telling to immortalize

a man who, like so many others, possessed far more wisdom than the world gave him credit for and was worth more than even he believed. This book is for you, my old friend. You were a wise spirit with no name, but I will never forget the lessons you taught me.

The Wisdom of an Unnamed Elder

This collection of sayings is a way to immortalize a man who possessed far more wisdom than the world gave him credit for. This book is for you, a world that desperately needs to hear from its elders, even the ones who are tired of talking.

Saying #1: The World's sweet poison offers visions of madness.

The world's sweet poison is the illusion of life created by a focus on materialism and separation from the natural world. This madness is a collective sickness that removes humanity from its spiritual roots. In many Native teachings, true wealth is measured not in possessions, but in the health of the community and the land. When we commodify nature—when a river is no longer a living relative but a resource to be dammed, or a forest is merely lumber to be sold—we sever a sacred connection. This disconnection creates a spiritual emptiness, a gnawing hunger for more that can never be satisfied because it is a hunger for the spiritual connection we have lost. The visions it offers are the false promises of comfort and fulfillment through conquest and accumulation. To live in a world consumed by this madness is to be perpetually off balance, to feel a constant anxiety born from straying from the sacred path. This wisdom is a call to awaken to a different way of being, one that recognizes the land as our first mother, the animals as our relatives, and the rivers as our blood, and to reject the illusion of a world that is "owned" in favor of a world that is loved and lived within. It is a fundamental truth that teaches us to see beyond the surface-level madness and reconnect with the reality of life.

Saying #2: Beat to the rhythm of your own drum, for every living thing has its own song.

This wisdom is a core principle of many Indigenous worldviews, a recognition that each individual, like every living thing, possesses a unique spirit and purpose. Just as the heartbeat of the Earth is echoed in the sacred drum, each person has an internal rhythm that guides their path. To "beat of your own drum" is to live authentically, in alignment with this sacred, internal song. It is a direct rejection of the fearful imitation and societal pressures that demand conformity. True freedom, in this context, is not an escape from responsibility but a dance of self-expression in harmony with the universe. It means surrendering the need to control life and instead allowing yourself to be carried by the natural flow of existence. This is the antithesis of the Western idea of conquest and domination. It is about trusting the universe and aligning your spirit with its movements. When a person is truly in rhythm with their own drum, their actions, thoughts, and words become clear and strong, without the static of the world's poison. This is the path of integrity, where one's life is a testament to the beautiful, unique song that the Creator placed within their spirit.

Saying #3: Impure motives poison all things.

The Native perspective on intention is that it is the spiritual root of any action. Just as a plant cannot produce healthy fruit from a poisoned root, an action cannot have a positive outcome if its motive is impure. This wisdom is a powerful check on the human heart, insisting on a constant self-examination of one's inner drive. An action, even one that seems good on the surface, is a form of pollution if it is rooted in selfishness, a desire for power, or personal gain. This applies to all aspects of life, from one's work to one's relationships.

The Elder's wisdom states that truth is the only pathway to a life of integrity, and that truth is measured not by words, but by actions. In many Native cultures, one's honor and standing are determined by their ability to "walk their talk." When we act from a place of service to others and a desire for balance in the world, our actions become a source of healing and positive creation.

But when our motives are impure, we contribute to the sickness within the world, no matter how outwardly successful or benevolent our actions may seem. This teaching is a call for radical honesty with oneself, a demand to constantly check the heart's true compass.

Saying #4: A good heart is sunlight for others.

In many Native traditions, a "good heart" is not a passive emotion but an active, conscious choice to be a force of positive change. The Elder's wisdom is that a good heart is "sunlight for others," a powerful medicine that combats the world's darkness. This is a rejection of the self-centeredness that can lead to spiritual sickness. A good heart is a warrior's choice to prioritize compassion and community well-being over personal gain. It manifests in small acts of kindness and in larger gestures of service to others, regardless of whether a person feels like a hero. It is the understanding that a person's value is not determined by their circumstances, but by their choices, especially the choice to act with generosity and love. It is the belief that even when an individual feels broken or purposeless, they still have the capacity to be a source of light for others.

In a world of imbalance, where the forces of greed and selfishness rage, a good heart is the most powerful medicine, and a reminder that the power of love and helping each other remains the only path forward.

Saying #5: A good heart is a warrior's choice.

The Native perspective on a good heart is that it is not a sign of weakness, but of a warrior's strength. This strength is found in the ability to overcome the greatest battle of all—the internal war against despair, anger, and the temptation to give in to the world's corrupting influences. A good heart is a conscious act of defiance against a world that has tried to break one's spirit. The Elder's wisdom is that this choice is an ongoing battle, one that must be fought daily. The true measure of a person lies not in the struggles they face, but in the choice to let their good heart guide their actions. A warrior with a good heart understands that true strength comes from integrity, humility, and the commitment to live in a sacred manner, even when it is the hardest path. A good heart is the most powerful shield against the poisons of the world, and it is the ultimate expression of a spirit that refuses to be conquered.

Saying #6: The word is a powerful force for creation and healing.

In Native traditions, the spoken word is not just a tool for communication; it is a sacred force with the power to shape reality. The Elder's wisdom is rooted in the oral traditions of his ancestors, where stories were told to keep a culture alive, prayers were spoken to call the rain, and blessings were offered to restore balance. Every word, he believed, has a spiritual energy that can be used for creation or destruction. It is a powerful tool for healing, capable of mending the soul and restoring harmony. The Elder saw this power firsthand, in the ceremonial languages that connected his people to the natural world. He understood that a person's words could build a world from nothing but a vision and a voice, and that honest words, rooted in truth, were the most powerful of all. This teaching is an invitation to use the word with intention and reverence, to choose words that bring life, light, and healing to the world and to the self. It is a fundamental truth that reminds us that we are co-creators with the universe.

Saying #7: Belief is a matter of survival, a living thing.

Belief, in Native tradition, is not a passive state but an active, living force that is essential for survival. It is a foundation that must be built with every thought and action, not simply a thing one says they possess. The Elder's wisdom reveals a truth that separates a flimsy belief of convenience from a foundational, unwavering one. A true belief is tested by fire, by the deepest forms of human suffering and despair. It is a matter of survival because it is the thread that connects a person to the Great Spirit and to the sacred path of the Red Road, even when all else seems lost. The Red Road is a path of integrity and spiritual living, and it is walked with every thought and every action. The Elder's teachings are a challenge to discard the superficial beliefs of the world and to build a belief system that is rooted in truth, a belief that is so strong it can weather any storm. This kind of belief is what gives a person the strength to "stay steady" in a world that is constantly trying to pull them off their path.

Saying #8: Freedom is a sacred dance on the path of truth.

In many Native traditions, freedom is a state of being, not a destination. It is a sacred dance, deeply tied to the rhythm of one's own drum and the natural flow of the universe. This is a stark contrast to the world's definition of freedom as a simple escape from pain or a lack of external rules. The Elder's wisdom teaches that true freedom is found by living in alignment with one's authentic purpose, on the path of truth. It is a continuous choice to live in balance and beauty with all things, to recognize the land as a living being, and to honor all of your relatives, human and otherwise.

For the Elder, this was a sacred dance, a defiant act against a world that had tried to strip him of his spirit. He knew that the only way to be truly free was to walk the narrow road of truth, to let go of the pain of the past, and to find liberation in the ongoing choice to live in a sacred manner.

This is the ultimate lesson of the warrior's heart—that a person can be in a metaphorical prison and still be free, and they can be seemingly free in the world and still be in a prison of their own making. True freedom is a state of spiritual liberation that can never be taken away.

Made in the USA
Coppell, TX
30 January 2026

70527204R00022